PRESENTED TO:

FROM:

DATE:

THE DETERMINED BOY

ISBN 978-1-7388789-0-1

THE DETERMINED BOY

A STORY BY

THADDEUS RAY
ELISABETH RAY
CATHERINE RAY
FELICITY RAY

This story is dedicated to our parents for being our best examples showing us that we should never give up even when times are hard.

❤ TR, ER, CR, FR

Hello Friend!

We made this book for a book exchange within our family. We wanted to gift a unique book to our parents as a way to show them that we see all that they do for us, and how they inspire us to give our best in everything!

In sharing this book with all of you, we are working through our mental blocks and fears of failure. We are putting ourselves before you as we practice our writing skills, and learn how to communicate values that are important to us.

We are learning that we can change the world with our unique differences. Even when things get hard, with determination and a positive attitude, we can be successful.

From the bottom of our hearts, we hope you enjoy this story as much as we enjoyed writing it. Don't let others limit what you can or cannot do. Give your best in everything, try and try again, and with practice you will find success!

May this be a blessings to you!

Thaddeus, Elisabeth, Catherine & Felicity

This is Jay. A well-mannered and polite 7-year-old boy who enjoys reading as much as playing soccer. Jay is born with a gift and a talent, but he doesn't know that yet.

Jay loves adventures. He is athletic, healthy, and smart. But being shorter than most children his age, he is often bullied for his height.

Schoolmates laugh at him as he walks by, pointing at him and calling him "Turtle Boy" because his backpack looked too big for his small body.

Bullies snatch his lunch, wave it over their heads, and jeer at him: "Shorty can't reach! Shorty can't reach!"

Jay was sad and frustrated. He cried his way home, not understanding why they picked on him. To let off steam, Jay spends most afternoons kicking his soccer ball all alone.

One day, he tried out for his school's soccer team, but they said that he was too short to play.

They let him join the team anyway, waiting for an opportunity to laugh at him when he falls or makes a mistake.

They would trip him on purpose, kick the ball way above his head, and make him feel lonely.

He had enough of it and decided to show them he has what it takes to be the best soccer player.

At home, he would study the moves of professional players, and then sprint around in the yard so he could be the fastest on the field. He was found kicking a soccer ball everywhere he went.

At tournaments, he was never chosen to start and was often a bench warmer.

Although he was often overlooked, that did not deter him from training hard and practicing on his own time. He showed up every day to practice and supported his team in any way he could.

When he did get to play, he was usually the last pick, and no one wanted to pass the ball to him.

But when he did get the ball, he always played his part as a team player, passing the ball with great accuracy and scoring when he had the opportunity.

His coach and teammates couldn't ignore his talents for long. Soon, he was in the starting lineup.

His determined attitude inspired his teammates, and it wasn't long before he was voted captain.

He kept his head in the game, never letting his newfound popularity distract him from giving his best at training and matches.

As he got older, he was offered sponsorships and scholarships. But life wasn't always handed to him. He still had to work hard and prove himself over and over again. There was always someone criticizing and discouraging.

Even as an adult, he faced judgment and challenges. Still, he kept fighting and was not disheartened. It only made him more determined.

Jay was doing this for himself and not to impress others.

Jay never let himself get too comfortable. He also didn't forget to be grateful for what he has achieved and experienced.

He likes looking back on what he had gone through and inspiring all he meets with stories from his childhood as the underdog.

Jay is proud of his never giving up attitude, trying and trying again even when life gets hard. He likes to remind everyone to be the best in whatever they choose to do!

Thaddeus (9), Elisabeth (7), Catherine (5), and Felicity (2) are four siblings who live on a farm in beautiful British Columbia, Canada. Be it rain, sun, or snow, hauling water, hay and chicken feed are part of their daily responsibilities. They are also self-motivated homeschoolers who enjoy reading, art, making music, and Brazilian Jiu Jitsu.

Thaddeus has a strong interest in history and all things military. He enjoys telling stories about war, reimagining battles and re-enacting them. He is also a keen builder of warships using recycled materials.

Thaddeus, 9

Elisabeth, 7

Elisabeth is an animal lover. She loves horses, and nurturing newborn chicks. When she's not reading about horses or out grooming her Shetland pony, Elisabeth can be found sketching horses. She also loves writing short stories on Mom's phone.

Catherine enjoys leaving thoughtful handwritten messages around the house, a real pick-me-up for those blessed enough to come upon them. An avid artist, Catherine enjoys drawing and painting the world around her.

Catherine, 5

Felicity, 2

Felicity may only be two at the time of publishing, but she is the epitome of determination. Full of wonder and energy, she often gets what she wants not because she is the baby of the family, but because she never gives up in pursuing the object of her desire.

www.ingramcontent.com/pod-product-compliance
Lightning Source LLC
LaVergne TN
LVHW021324160826
845679LV00001B/464

* 9 7 8 1 7 3 8 8 7 8 9 0 1 *